Junk Food, Yes or No

Bonnie Carole

Rourke
Educational Media

rourkeeducationalmedia.com

Scan for Related Titles
and Teacher Resources

Teaching Focus:

Using Expression- Have students read aloud to practice reading with expression and with appropriate pacing.

Before Reading:

Building Academic Vocabulary and Background Knowledge

Before reading a book, it is important to set the stage for your child or students by using pre-reading strategies. This will help them develop their vocabulary, increase their reading comprehension, and make connections across the curriculum.

1. *Read the title and look at the cover. Let's make predictions about what this book will be about.*
2. *Take a picture walk by talking about the pictures/photographs in the book. Implant the vocabulary as you take the picture walk. Be sure to talk about the text features such as headings, Table of Contents, glossary, bolded words, captions, charts/diagrams, or Index.*
3. *Have students read the first page of text with you then have students read the remaining text.*
4. *Strategy Talk – use to assist students while reading.*
   - *Get your mouth ready*
   - *Look at the picture*
   - *Think…does it make sense*
   - *Think…does it look right*
   - *Think…does it sound right*
   - *Chunk it – by looking for a part you know*
5. *Read it again.*
6. *After reading the book complete the activities below.*

Content Area Vocabulary
Use glossary words in a sentence.
argue
issue
nutritional
opponents
proponents
spoil

After Reading:

Comprehension and Extension Activity

After reading the book, work on the following questions with your child or students in order to check their level of reading comprehension and content mastery.

1. *Why is it important to think about what you eat? (Summarize)*
2. *What are some healthy items you eat at lunch? What are some unhealthy items? (Text to self connection)*
3. *What foods are considered to be junk foods? (Summarize)*
4. *How can food labels help you make decisions on what to eat? (Asking questions)*

Extension Activity

What kinds of foods are you eating? Are you making sure you are eating a fruit, vegetable, grain, protein, and dairy item for each meal? Plan a meal for your family. What would it look like? Draw a picture of your meal and label which foods are fruit, vegetable, grain, protein, and dairy items. Are all the items healthy items? Is your entire meal considered healthy?

Table of Contents

Introduction

"I can eat pizza every day!"

"An apple a day keeps the doctor away!"

Everyone has different opinions about junk food. But what is junk food? Junk food has few nutrients and is usually high in sugar, salt, and fat.

Salty snacks, desserts, fried fast food, and sugary drinks are considered junk foods.

Your opinion is how you feel about something. People can have different opinions about an **issue**. What do you think about junk food?

Arguments for Junk Food

Proponents of junk food say that eating it is okay. They **argue** that there are reasons to have junk food.

Junk food can help raise money for field trips, sports teams, or other programs. Many people will buy cookies or candy bars to support a fundraiser.

Packaging and a long shelf-life can make cookies and candy easy to buy, sell, and store.

What healthy foods do you have at home right now? Fruits and vegetables can be more expensive and **spoil** more quickly than processed foods.

Fresh produce and meats need to be eaten much sooner than a bag of chips.

Do you have after-school activities that keep you out late? Sometimes there isn't time to cook a fresh meal. Fast food restaurants can make life easier for families.

Proponents of junk food say people should have a choice in what they eat. They say junk food should be an option for people who like it.

children's Menu

Grilled Chicken Salad..............$10.00
Cheeseburger.....................$10.00
Grilled Fish.........................$10.00
Pizza $10.00
Chicken Fingers....................$10.00

Choices are a part of growing up. Learning to make choices is important. What kind of choices would you make at a restaurant?

Are chicken nuggets unhealthy? Is pizza? How about apple pie? People may not agree on what foods are healthy and unhealthy. The way food is prepared can make a difference.

Nutrition Facts

Serving Size 2 oz (56g - about 1/7 box)
Servings Per Container about 7

Amount Per Serving

Calories 200	Calories from Fat 15

	% Daily Value*
Total Fat 6.5g	**2%**
Saturated Fat 4g	**0%**
Trans Fat 2g	
Cholesterol 0mg	**0%**
Sodium 10mg	**0%**
Total Carbohydrate 41g	**14%**
Dietary Fiber 6g	**24%**
Sugars 2g	
Protein 7g	

Most foods have easy-to-read labels that list calories, sugar, and fat counts. These labels help people choose what to eat.

Arguments against Junk Food

Do you choose vegetables over candy? Junk food **opponents** say junk foods can cause health problems.

How do you feel after eating junk food? Unhealthy foods can make you feel tired. They may lack important nutrients your body needs to function throughout the day.

Can you eat more apples or potato chips before feeling full? Junk food has little **nutritional** value. Some ingredients can make you feel hungrier. Eating large amounts of junk food can contribute to obesity.

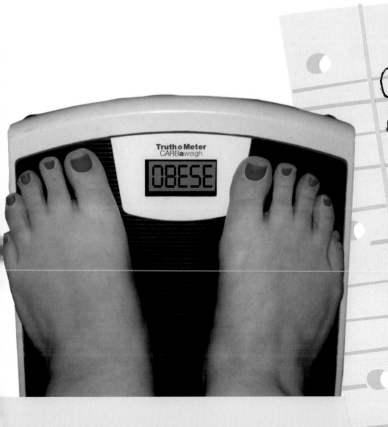

Obesity is when a person has too much body fat. Your body fat is measured through your body mass index (BMI). BMI is calculated using your height, weight, and gender.

Did you know that what you eat as a child can affect you when you're an adult? Junk food can contribute to health problems such as diabetes in adults and children.

People with diabetes must monitor their blood sugar levels by drawing blood every day.

Bad fats in junk food can replace the healthy fats in the brain. This can slow down a person's ability to learn.

There's a link between nutritious foods and school performance. Experts say better nutrition can lead to better students.

Do you know how much sugar is in your favorite drink? A large amount of sugar is common in junk food. Sugar can lead to bad oral health, including rotten teeth and stinky breath.

You Decide

What side are you on? What are your arguments about junk food? You can share what you think in many ways. One way is by writing an opinion paper.

Writing Tips

- Tell your opinion first. Use phrases such as:
  - *I like* _____. *both*
  - *I think* _____. *fruit*
  - _____ *is the best* _____. *drink*

- Give many reasons to support your opinion. Use facts instead of stating your feelings.

- Use the words *and, because,* and *also* to connect your opinion to your reasons.

- Explain your facts by using phrases, such as *for example,* or *such as*.

- Compare your opinion to a different opinion. Then point out reasons your opinion is better. You can use phrases such as:
  - *Some people think,* _____ *but I disagree because* _____.
  - _____ *is better than* _____ *because* _____.

- Give examples of the positive outcomes of someone agreeing with your opinion. For example, you can use the phrase: *If* _____ *then* _____.

- Include a short story about your own experiences with the topic. For example, if you are persuading someone that the best pet is a dog, you can talk about your pet dog.

- Restate your opinion so your reader remembers how you feel.

Glossary

argue (ahr-gyoo): to give your opinion
about something

issue (ish-oo): main topic for debate or discussion

nutritional (noo-trish-uhn-al): something
that nourishes

opponents (uh-poh-nuhnts): people who are not in
favor, or argue against something

proponents (pro-po-nuhnts): people who argue for
or support something

spoil (spoil): to become rotten or unfit for eating

Index

Show What You Know

1. How does junk food affect your oral health?
2. What types of foods are considered junk food?
3. How can after-school activities affect what you eat?

Websites to Visit

www.diabetes.org/diabetes-basics/type-1

www.nourishinteractive.com/kids

www.foodchamps.org

About the Author

Bonnie Carole enjoys junk food at sporting events and festivals. Her favorites are pretzels and funnel cakes. She and her family try to eat healthy. She even feeds her dogs vegetables like green beans and carrots!

Meet The Author!
www.meetREMauthors.com

www.rourkeeducationalmedia.com

PHOTO CREDITS: Cover (left): ©Celig; cover (right): ©Maryna Kulchytska; page 1: ©Monkey Business Images; page 4: ©Cristian Baitig; page 5: ©GlobalStock; page 6: ©Funwithfood; page 7: ©Catherine Lane; page 8: ©ac_bnphotos; page 9: ©PavelLPhotoand Video; page 10: ©Whiteart; page 11: ©Alinute Silzeviciute; page 12: ©svanhorn; page 13: ©Ines Bazdar; page 14: ©StaffordStudios; page 15: ©JENEK22; page 16: ©AMR Images; page 17: ©BraunS; page 18: ©Rob Hyrons; page 19: ©ferhatMatt; page 19: ©wckiw; page 20: ©Pamela A. Moore

Edited by: Keli Sipperley
Cover and Interior design by: Rhea Magaro

Library of Congress PCN Data

Junk Food, Yes or No/Bonnie Carole
(Seeing Both Sides)
ISBN (hard cover)(alk. paper) 978-1-63430-350-7
ISBN (soft cover) 978-1-63430-450-4
ISBN (e-Book) 978-1-63430-549-5
Library of Congress Control Number: 2015931679

Printed in the United States of America, North Mankato, Minnesota

Also Available as:
ROURKE'S
e-Books